A Story of Mother Elizabeth Seton

By
Brother Ernest, C.S.C.

Pictures by
Carolyn Lee Jagodits

Neumann Press
Gastonia, North Carolina

Nihil Obstat:

    C.F. Brooks, C.S.C.

        Censor Deputatus

Cum Permissu:

    Brother Donatus Schmitz, C.S.C

        Provincial

Imprimatur:

    †Most Rev. Leo A. Pursley, D.D.

        Bishop of Fort Wayne-South Bend

First Printing 1960

A Story of Mother Elizabeth Seton

ISBN: 978-1-5051-2102-5

Printed and bound in the United States of America.

Neumann Press
Gastonia, North Carolina
www.TANBooks.com
2021

To Brother Richard Shea, C.S.C.

A STORY OF MOTHER ELIZABETH SETON

Elizabeth Ann Bayley, who is known to all of us as Mother Elizabeth Seton, was born in New York on a terribly hot August day in 1774.

Her daddy was Doctor Richard Bayley, famous for his loving care of the sick, and for the intense study he was making of croup, a disease which in those days, and for many years thereafter, made life miserable for thousands. Doctor Bayley even went to England to study under a famous doctor there who was making some progress toward a cure for this disease.

Doctor Bayley was in London at the time when the American colonies issued their Declaration of Independence. He knew that would mean war, for England would not sit back and let the control of this nation slip from her. And the doctor at that time was sympathetic to England.

So, Doctor Bayley signed up as a surgeon in the British army and set sail for America. It took two weeks to make the crossing, and he was met at the boat by his wife and two daughters. They were delighted to see him, but as soon as they heard he was to go on at once and join General Howe's army in Newport, Rhode Island, their gladness ended quickly.

"I'm sorry I must go so soon, my dear," said Doctor Bayley, but I feel sure that the war will not last very long!"

Some days later, Mrs. Bayley with her two
beautiful daughters accompanied Doctor Bayley
to the station where he was to leave for Newport. It was a sad parting for all, but especially
for Mrs. Bayley who was always fearful for her
husband's health when he was away from her.
She knew that when he got absorbed in his work, he
gave no thought to himself.

Early in the spring of 1777 another daughter was born to Dr. and Mrs. Bayley. War conditions prevented the doctor from coming home to see his little daughter. Mrs. Bayley understood, and since she and her daughter were both getting along well, she did not beg for him to come.

A couple of months later, however, a letter did come to camp for Doctor Dick, as his men loved to call him. It begged for him to come at once for his wife was dying!

Doctor Bayley at once got permission to resign from Howe's army and hurried back to his home in Newtown, New York.

A few days after his arrival, and in spite of all he and other doctors could do, his good wife died, leaving behind her a brokenhearted husband, and three young daughters, too young to fully realize their loss.

One of the things Mrs. Bayley had begged her husband to do was to remarry so that the children would have the care they really needed.

So, after a year of mourning, Doctor Bayley married Charlotte Barclay. Miss Barclay loved the doctor's children, and after the marriage, she gave them all of her love and attention.

When Elizabeth was old enough, she went to a private school where her favorite subjects were French and music. She learned to speak and write the language well. And all who heard her play the piano agreed she was a real musician.

Elizabeth was nine years old when the war for independence was finally over and the English left our country. And she was very happy to learn that her parents decided to remain in New York, and her father would continue his medical practice. Peace was what she wanted.

Through the years that followed, seven children were born to Dr. and Mrs. Bayley. Because of the amount of care the children required, Elizabeth began to feel lonely in her own home.

But this changed one evening in 1793 when, at a party, Elizabeth met a wonderful young man by the name of William Seton. And by the time that party was over, Elizabeth was deeply in love!

From time to time after that, Elizabeth met William. She learned that he had been educated in England, and that he was a violinist. She was glad that he loved music, and asked him to bring his violin along when he came to visit her.

The first time they played together, each became convinced of the other's talent, and before long these musical evenings were shared by many of Doctor Bayley's friends.

About a year after Elizabeth first met William Seton, she agreed to marry him. Both were in favor of a small, private, wedding celebration, with just a few of their friends present. So, it was agreed that the wedding would take place on January 24, in the home of her sister, Mary, who was already married to Doctor Wright Post.

Since both Elizabeth and William belonged to the Anglican church, and both were very important families in the city, they asked Bishop Provost to witness their marriage.

After their wedding, the young Mr. and Mrs. Seton went to live with William's father until their own home on Wall Street was completed.

It was autumn when their beautiful home was ready, but Elizabeth was already worrying about her husband. For some time now, William had been coughing heavily, and the doctor had not been able to do anything for him. It was feared that he had tuberculosis. He had long since been advised by his doctor to take a long rest, or at least to slow down, but since he was working for a firm that was making great progress, he felt that he needed to be on the job so that no one would be given his place.

"Your health is more important than your job, dear," said Elizabeth. We have plenty."

On May 3, 1795, Elizabeth Seton gave birth to a beautiful daughter whom she named Anna Maria. William had hoped that their first baby would be a boy so that he would grow up and take over much of his work, and be able to care for Elizabeth if, as the doctors were telling him, he would not live long. But William said nothing about his disappointment.

Little Anna Maria was able to walk and to get into everything when, on November 25, 1796, God sent her a little baby brother. This bouncing youngster was given the name of William after his proud father.

"And he has your good looks, too," said Elizabeth, teasing her idolizing husband.

"If he has your good heart, dear, I'll be perfectly satisfied. It's more important than looks."

Had it not been for William's cough, Elizabeth Seton felt she could not be happier. The firm of Seton, Maitland and Company was thriving in both America and Europe, and they were able to have everything that makes life pleasant.

Suddenly, however, in 1798, as Elizabeth was about to give birth to another baby, word came of the death of William's father. It was a great shock to both Elizabeth and her husband.

"Besides our great loss, my dear, this means that I will have to take over dad's work, and you will have to care for his six children!"

"We will have to think about that later. At present, I can hardly care for myself," teased Elizabeth.

While giving birth to her baby, both mother and child nearly died, and it was many months before any serious thought could be given to anything but to them.

But when her strength did return, Elizabeth moved her family into the Seton home on Stone Street and she and William's sister, Rebecca, began the work of raising nine children!

And to make matters worse, her husband soon found out he had not the ability his father had, for already business was beginning to slow down. There were reasons for worry, indeed.

The arrival of their fourth child in June of 1800 did nothing at all to raise the gloom that had descended upon William Seton.

Two months later, everyone knew that the great firm of Seton, Maitland and Company was bankrupt, and all were shocked at the news.

"Imagine, dear, everything gone in just two years after father's death!" sobbed William.

"Don't say we have lost everything, William. It is not as bad as that. The important thing right now is for you to care for your health."

"I cannot rest now, Elizabeth. I must do what I can to save some of the business."

Elizabeth knew it was useless to push her point. Always one to pray, she turned more and more to God for help. And she needed all she could get.

During the hot month of August of 1801, Dr. Bayley became ill from overwork. Elizabeth hurried to him and remained at his side until he died. Then, heartbroken, she returned to her children and the many charitable employments she had assumed in the city.

The following summer, Elizabeth's fifth child was born — a little girl she named Rebecca. She seemed a healthy baby and delighted both her parents. And they really needed that joy!

William's health was failing fast. Elizabeth felt that he should go to Italy where the climate often helps those suffering from lung trouble.

After much thought, William agreed to go if Elizabeth and Anna Maria went along. So, arrangements were made for the care of the other children, and the voyage was begun.

When their boat docked in Leghorn, they were told that, because of the yellow fever epidemic in America, they would have to remain in quarantine for thirty days. During that time William often seemed close to death.

When they were released from the hospital, they went to Pisa, and there, only ten days later, William Seton died!

During the months she had to wait for the boat to take her back to America, Elizabeth and Anna Maria lived with some Catholic friends in Italy.

"I think you would enjoy reading this," said Mr. Filicchi, her host, handing Elizabeth a life of St. Francis de Sales.

"I shall be happy to read it," said Elizabeth as she looked at the title of the book.

When Elizabeth finished reading the book she got on her knees and begged God to enlighten her and give her the help needed to do His Will.

It was not until June 4, 1804, that Elizabeth and Anna Maria got back to New York and her family. She was amazed at how her children had grown during her absence. And it was now up to her to provide for them.

Elizabeth did not forget her friends, the Filicchis and the introduction they had given her to Catholicism. After she had her home running smoothly again, she began to take instructions in the Faith, and early in 1805 she and her children were baptized.

Her joy was so great on the day she made her First Communion that she had to share it with the Filicchis. She wrote them a long letter thanking them for what they had done for her, and of her great desire to live her life in conformity with Christ's wishes as expressed in the Bible and in the teaching of the Church.

Mr. Filicchi then wrote a letter to his friend, Bishop John Carroll of Baltimore, telling him about her and her works of charity. The bishop already knew of Mrs. Seton and her works of charity and looked forward to even greater things.

The good bishop then got in touch with Elizabeth and learned from her that she now had to live with her sister because she could not afford a home of her own. She also told him that most of her friends had turned against her since she had become a Catholic.

Bishop Carroll at once sent Elizabeth's sons, William and Richard, to Georgetown College. That was a great relief for her. Then she decided to rent a house and take in boarders. In that way she hoped to support herself and family. But the venture did not work. She had to give it up. She might have to depend upon charity!

But God was watching over the Setons, and He sent Father Dubourg, president of St. Mary's College in Baltimore, to talk to her.

"I would like you to come to Baltimore and open a school for girls near our college. I will give you the land, and I promise you will always have plenty of students!"

Elizabeth agreed to move to Baltimore.

When her school opened for the first time, Mrs. Seton had four young ladies and her two daughters as students. She was happy.

Soon after this she got an idea to found a religious Community to help her in this work.

One morning after Holy Communion she heard within her a voice telling her to see Mr. Cooper and that he would give her property and needed assistance. She at once went to see Father Dubourg and told him what had happened. The good priest knew no one by that name, but a few hours later a Mr. Cooper came to Father Dubourg.

Mr. Cooper was from Emmitsburg, a town not far from Baltimore. He wanted to give fifty million francs for the building of a school for girls in his city. And he further amazed the good priest by telling him that the work started in Emmitsburg would then spread everywhere!

Mr. Cooper bought a good piece of property in Emmitsburg and gave it to Mrs. Seton. He then entered a seminary to study for the priesthood.

Elizabeth then went on with the idea of founding a Community and decided to call her spiritual daughters the Sisters of Charity of St. Joseph.

In March of 1809, Elizabeth took private vows of poverty, chastity, and obedience, and began to live as a religious. Others soon joined her, and she suggested that they all follow the Rule Saint Vincent de Paul had written for his Daughters of Charity.

The Sisters then decided to wear the garments widows wore in those days, such as Elizabeth had worn since her husband's death. It consisted of a little white bonnet which covered the hair, a black dress which fell in folds almost to the ground, and a short black cape.

The first house of the Sisters of Charity in Emmitsburg was made of logs. It had only three rooms, but it was a beginning. More young ladies soon came to share Mother Seton's poverty and her work. And God tried her by taking her two daughters, Anna Maria and Rebecca, after long and painful illnesses. She continued to pray that God would call her sons to the priesthood.

The number of ladies who came to join Elizabeth increased, and in 1814 she was able to send three to open an orphanage in Philadelphia. The next year she sent Sisters to care for the infirmary of St. Mary's College, Baltimore. In 1817 we find them in New York conducting an orphanage and a school. God was indeed blessing Mother Seton's efforts, but He was already warning her that her stay on earth was going to be short.

In 1820, she had to tell her spiritual daughters that the disease that had carried off her husband was already progressing rapidly in herself. The pain she felt in her chest was now so severe that she had to spend most of her time in bed. But she was happy that she was given more time for prayer. There was so much to be thankful for, and so many favors she wanted for her young Community, already serving God in many places.

On January 4, 1821, Mother Seton asked for and received the Last Sacraments. She was very calm and cheerful. She asked to have the Sisters come to her room. When they arrived, she humbly asked them to forgive her if she had ever offended them. Then she begged them to love one another and to try their best to observe the Rule she had given them. A little smile spread over her beautiful face, and Mother Elizabeth Seton breathed her last.

From her place in heaven, Mother Seton still watches over her Community as it continues to spread over the world.

The End